Human Living Systems

Heredity

Karen Bledsoe

Perfection Learning®

Editorial Director: Susan C. Thies
Editor: Mary L. Bush
Design Director: Randy Messer
Book Design: Brian Shearer, Tobi Cunningham
Cover Design: Michael A. Aspengren

A special thanks to the following for his scientific review of the book:
Paul Pistek, Instructor of Biological Sciences,
North Iowa Area Community College

Image credits:
©Photononstop/CORBIS: pp. 2–3; ©Jim Craigmyle/CORBIS: p. 9; ©Bettmann/CORBIS: p. 10; ©Perinn Pierre/CORBIS SYGMA: p. 15; ©Digital Art/CORBIS: p. 17; ©Royalty-Free/CORBIS: p. 26 (top); ©Andrew Brookes/CORBIS: p. 33; ©Chris Stewart/San Francisco Chronicle/CORBIS: p. 36; ©Ariel Skelley/CORBIS: p. 40

Photos.com: front cover, all left/right page backgrounds, pp. 1, 4, 5 (bottom), 6–7 (bottom), 7 (top), 22, 27; Istock.com: back cover, pp. 5 (top), 6 (foreground), 8, 12, 13, 14, 16–17 (background), 18–19 (background), 20, 23, 25, 26 (bottom), 28, 30, 31, 35; ©Jane Ades, NHGRI: p. 32; Perfection Learning Corporation: pp. 16, 18, 19, 29, 34

Text © 2007 by Perfection Learning® Corporation.
All rights reserved. No part of this book may be reproduced, stored in a retrieval system, or transmitted in any form or by any means, electronic, mechanical, photocopying, recording, or otherwise, without prior permission of the publisher. Printed in the United States of America.

For information, contact
Perfection Learning® Corporation
1000 North Second Avenue, P.O. Box 500
Logan, Iowa 51546-0500.
Phone: 1-800-831-4190
Fax: 1-800-543-2745
perfectionlearning.com

1 2 3 4 5 6 PP 12 11 10 09 08 07

PB ISBN 0-7891-7016-7
RLB ISBN 0-7569-6643-4

Table of Contents

1. Family Pictures 4
2. Heredity History 8
3. The Essential Elements of Heredity 14
4. Inheritance Information 21
5. Mutations 29
6. New Genetic Frontiers 31

Internet Connections and Related Reading
for Heredity 37

Glossary 38

Index 40

chapter one

Family Pictures

Have you ever looked at a family picture and wondered why each of you looks like you do? You have your mother's eyes and nose. You're tall like your father. Your sister, on the other hand, looks almost nothing like you. She's short and has curly hair and blue eyes. It seems impossible that she even came from the same family.

Most families are like yours. They show a mix of **traits** that sometimes appears to make sense but other times seems surprising. How does this happen? The answer lies in **heredity**. Heredity is the process by which traits are passed down from one generation to the next.

Traits are characteristics that people possess. Many traits are inherited, or passed down, from family members. Most of your physical features, such as eye color, hair color, and height, are inherited traits. Certain diseases or a **predisposition** to certain diseases are also traits you acquire through heredity.

Caution!

Not all traits are due strictly to heredity. Environment also plays a role in many of your traits. For example, you may inherit natural athletic, musical, or intellectual abilities, but if you don't practice and develop your skills, they won't become strong traits. You may inherit fair skin, but if you spend a lot of time in the Sun, it may darken. And while you may inherit a tendency for heart disease, a healthy diet, exercise, and stress management may change your chances of actually getting the disease. So be careful not to blame all of your traits on heredity!

Genetics

Genetics is the science of heredity. Geneticists carry out research to understand how traits such as hair color and nose shape are passed on from parents to children. They study the patterns that occur in inherited traits. Understanding genetics can help *you* understand why you look like you do!

chapter two

Heredity
History

For centuries, people have noticed that children, calves, puppies, and other **offspring** seemed to inherit a mix of traits from their parents. Before anyone understood the science of heredity, people tried different explanations of how inheritance worked.

Blood Relatives?

Have you ever said that sports were "in your blood"? Or maybe on St. Patrick's Day, you're proud of the fact that you have "Irish blood." Where do these expressions come from? Long ago, ancient philosophers believed that traits were controlled by liquid factors in blood. Aristotle thought that when a substance from a mother and a substance from a father blended together in the blood of offspring, it created the blending of traits seen in the child. This seemed to explain, for instance, why a parent with fair skin and a parent with dark skin could have a child with medium-toned skin.

Purely Unpredictable?

There were some problems, however, with the idea of traits blending through blood. People began to observe that all traits are not a "blend" of other traits. Earlobes, for example, can be free or attached. There are no blended "half-attached" earlobes. Also, some traits, such as red hair, could skip one or two generations entirely. So a mother with blond hair and a father with brown hair may have a child with red hair. These observations led some people to believe that the inheritance of traits was totally unpredictable.

The Father of Genetics

In the middle of the 19th century, a monk in Moravia developed a better explanation of heredity. Gregor Mendel was a farmer's son. He joined the Catholic church to get an education. He ended up teaching and helping other monks grow crops. He developed a special interest in understanding how traits are inherited by plants.

Mendel studied inheritance in pea plants. He spent years **crossbreeding** hundreds of pea plants and observing thousands of offspring. He discovered that traits such as stem height, seed color, and flower color were passed on from parent to offspring in predictable patterns. Furthermore, the traits he observed were never blended in the offspring. For example, the seeds were always yellow or green, never yellow-green. This suggested that traits were not passed on by a blending of liquids but by some type of individual "particle."

Gregor Mendel

Pea Plant Traits

Trait	Dominant Expression	Recessive Expression
seed color	yellow	green
seed form	smooth	wrinkled
pod color	green	yellow
pod shape	inflated	constricted/pinched
flower color	purple	white
flower position	axial (between stem and leaf)	terminal (at the end of stem)
stem height	tall	short/dwarf

Mendel began his experiments with plants that bred true for particular traits, such as those that always produced the same color flowers. When Mendel crossed purple-flowered plants with white-flowered plants, the offspring all had purple flowers. But when he crossed these purple-flowered offspring with one another, three-fourths of the next generation had purple flowers and one-fourth had white flowers. The white-flower trait had not gone away, nor was it blended with the purple trait. Mendel reasoned that the plants in the second generation each had one hereditary particle for the purple-flower trait and one for the white-flower trait. When two of these plants crossed, they could give either the purple or the white particle to their offspring.

Mendel concluded that the individual particles must be what passed on traits from generation to generation. He called these particles *elementen*. Today Mendel's elementen are known as **genes**. Mendel realized that these genes must come in pairs. In offspring, one gene comes from the "father" parent plant and the other comes from the "mother" parent plant.

Mendel also recognized that some genes were **dominant** and some were **recessive**. Dominant genes overpowered other genes and determined what trait the plant exhibited. Recessive genes were only visible when no dominant ones were present. Recessive genes seemed to "disappear" when dominant genes took over but came back if paired with another recessive gene. In the case of the pea plants, the purple-flower gene was dominant. If a plant had two purple-flower genes, the flowers were purple. If a plant had two white-flower genes, the flowers were white. If a plant had one purple and one white gene, the dominant purple gene overruled the recessive white one and the flowers were purple.

Prove It with Punnett Squares

Punnett squares are used to show the possible combinations of genes that parents can pass down to their offspring. They also show the probability that each offspring will have of expressing the different traits. This Punnett square shows the possible combinations of genes for two pea plants that carry a dominant smooth-seed gene (S) and a recessive wrinkled-seed gene (s). The offspring will have a 75 percent chance (3 in 4) of having smooth seeds and a 25 percent chance (1 in 4) of having wrinkled seeds.

From Mendel to Modern Genetics

Mendel published his work in the mid-1860s, but it was mostly ignored. Then in 1900, years after his death, his work was rediscovered by three different scientists. Hugo de Vries, Carl Correns, and Erich Tschermak were botanists studying the patterns of heredity among plants. All of them came to conclusions similar to Mendel's, helping establish what became known as Mendel's Laws of Heredity. These laws became the basis for modern genetics.

chapter three

The Essential Elements of Heredity

Gregor Mendel proposed the existence of small hereditary particles called *elementen*. At the time, many people doubted these particles existed because no one could see them. However, tools and technology in the 20th century made it easier to identify the essential elements of heredity—**DNA**, genes, and **chromosomes**.

DNA

DNA, or deoxyribonucleic acid, is found in the center (nucleus) of every cell in the human body. DNA is a long molecule that helps in the production of **proteins**. Proteins are responsible for a body's formation, growth, repair, and reproduction. They control all of the basic functions in a body.

Every person's DNA is different. Only identical siblings (twins, triplets, etc.) have the same DNA.

The first model of DNA was completed in 1953 by Francis Crick and James Watson. The two scientists had help from another scientist, Maurice Wilkins. Wilkins recognized the important role that X-rays could play in viewing DNA.

Watson and Crick

Scientist of Significance

Watson and Crick are credited for discovering the structure of DNA, but they could never have constructed their model without data collected by Rosalind Franklin.

Franklin was a British chemist who used X-rays to study crystallized molecules. In 1951, she began working as a research assistant at King's College in London in the same lab where Maurice Wilkins worked. Wilkins was already working on DNA and thought that Franklin would help him. Instead, she was assigned the DNA X-ray work while he was on vacation and it became her project. The two scientists then became rivals.

Franklin worked on various forms of DNA for two years, producing some spectacular X-ray pictures. She made several speculations about the makeup of DNA and came quite close to discovering its structure herself. But she had no collaborators to work with, so her progress was slow. Wilkins, on the other hand, was constantly collaborating with Watson and Crick.

Still, Franklin might have been the first to describe the structure of DNA had Wilkins not shared some of Franklin's X-rays with Watson and Crick without her knowledge. Watson and Crick used this information to finish their model and publish their results.

In 1962, Watson, Crick, and Wilkins shared the Nobel Prize for Medicine for their work with DNA. Sadly, Franklin had already died of cancer in 1958.

Crick and Watson's model showed that DNA is shaped like a twisted ladder called a *double helix*. The sides of the ladder are formed from deoxyribose sugar and **phosphates**. The rungs are formed by four molecules called **bases**. The four bases are adenine, thymine, guanine, and cytosine. Bases pair up to form rungs of the DNA ladder. Adenine is always matched with thymine, while guanine is always matched with cytosine. The order in which pairs of bases are lined up in a DNA molecule forms the code that tells a cell how to make all of the proteins it needs.

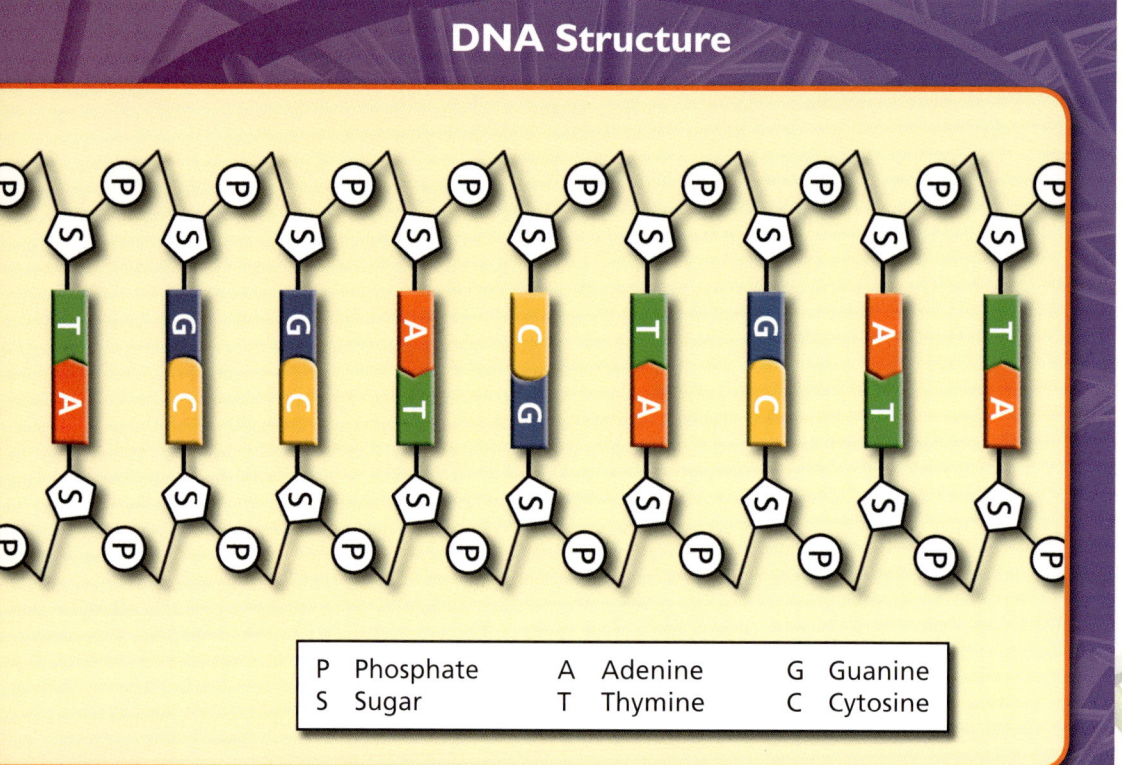

DNA Structure

| P Phosphate | A Adenine | G Guanine |
| S Sugar | T Thymine | C Cytosine |

Tracing the Path of Science

The base-pairing rule was first proposed by Ernest Chargaff in 1950. Chargaff chemically analyzed DNA and found that there are always equal amounts of adenine and thymine and equal amounts of cytosine and guanine. Chargaff hypothesized that the bases must pair up with their similar partners. Chargaff explained his findings to Watson and Crick in 1952. The men then used Chargaff's rule when they built their DNA molecule the next year.

Once the structure of DNA was discovered, other scientists studied how DNA worked. They found that when cells divide, DNA molecules copy themselves, passing on the same genetic codes that the original cells contained. Genes play a big role in this process.

Genes

A gene is a segment of DNA that contains the code, or instructions, for making a certain protein. Humans have 20,000 to 25,000 genes. These genes determine what traits a person will have.

DNA is like a library of rare books. Rather than let books leave the library, when someone needs information found on a page of a book, a librarian just makes a copy of it. In the same way, when a cell needs a particular protein, just the gene that's needed is copied. This copy is made from another acid called **RNA** (ribonucleic acid).

To copy a gene, the two sides of the DNA ladder of the gene are "unzipped." RNA bases move in to match up with the exposed bases on one side of the DNA ladder. RNA lacks the base thymine, but it has a similar base called *uracil*. Uracil matches with adenine just as thymine does. The RNA molecule that's formed from the copying process is called *mRNA* or *messenger RNA*.

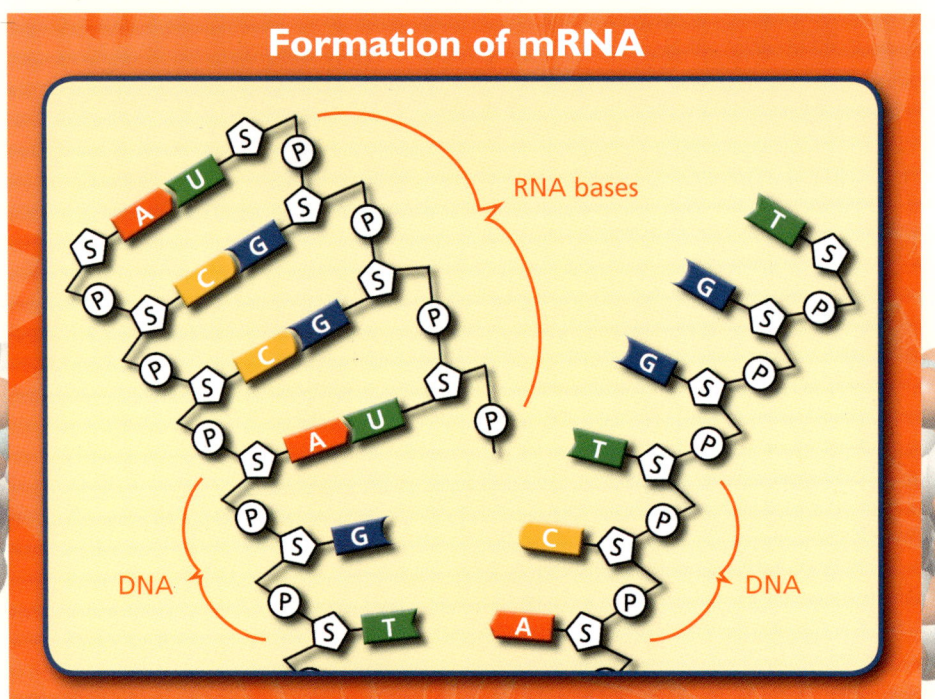

Formation of mRNA

The mRNA is released into the cell's **cytoplasm**. Here it attaches to a **ribosome**. The ribosome reads the instructions coded in the mRNA and produces a matching protein.

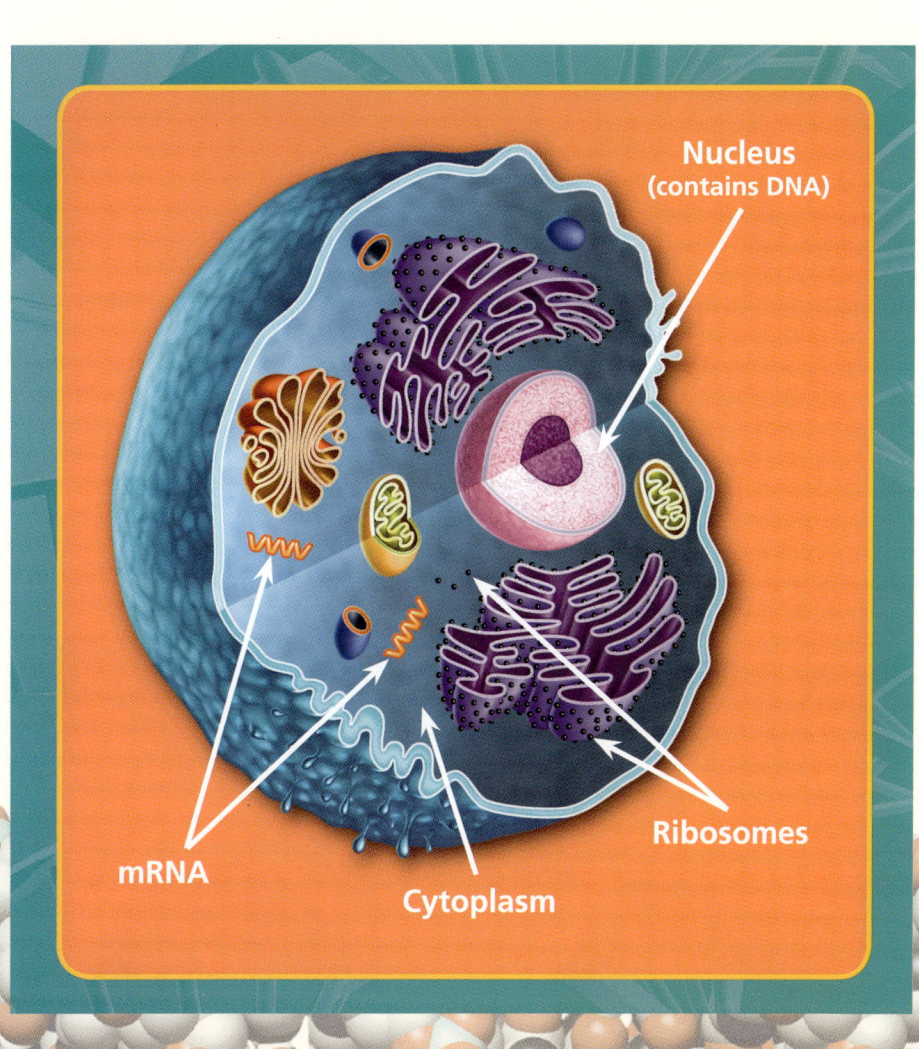

Chromosomes

Genes are located on chromosomes. Chromosomes are structures found in a cell's nucleus. Each rod-shaped chromosome can have up to several thousand genes lined up on it. Human chromosomes come in pairs. One member of each pair comes from the father, and the other comes from the mother. There are a total of 46 chromosomes, or 23 pairs, in all.

One pair of chromosomes in humans determines whether an offspring will be male or female. These chromosomes are known as the **sex chromosomes**. Females have a pair of X sex chromosomes. Males have one X and one Y sex chromosome. When a male and female each pass on one of their sex chromosomes to an offspring, the female always contributes an X chromosome. The male contributes either an X or a Y chromosome, determining whether the offspring will be a girl or a boy.

Inheritance Information

chapter four

Gregor Mendel discovered several key factors in heredity, but his work didn't explain all of the components of human genetics. Today scientists know that traits can be determined by a single gene or many different genes. They also recognize several basic patterns of inherited traits.

Alleles

Genes have different forms. These forms are called **alleles**. Some genes have just two alleles. Other genes have more than two alleles. This is referred to as "multiple alleles." Even if a gene has multiple alleles, any one person has only two of these alleles (one from each parent). These two alleles will determine what trait the offspring has.

Two-Allele Traits

Dominant	Recessive
curling tongue	noncurling tongue
full lips	thin lips
freckles	no freckles
farsightedness	normal vision
connected eyebrows	separate eyebrows
straight thumb	hitchhiker's (bent) thumb

21

Complete Dominance

What Mendel discovered was a pattern of inheritance called *complete dominance*. This means that the dominant allele of a gene always dominates completely over the recessive allele.

Earlobe shape in humans is controlled by a single gene with two alleles. One allele produces earlobes that hang free. This is the dominant form of the gene. The other allele produces attached earlobes. This is the recessive form of the gene. Every offspring inherits one copy of the earlobe gene from each parent. If a person inherits two alleles for free earlobes or one free and one attached allele, the person will have free-hanging earlobes. Only if a person inherits two alleles for attached earlobes will the person have attached earlobes.

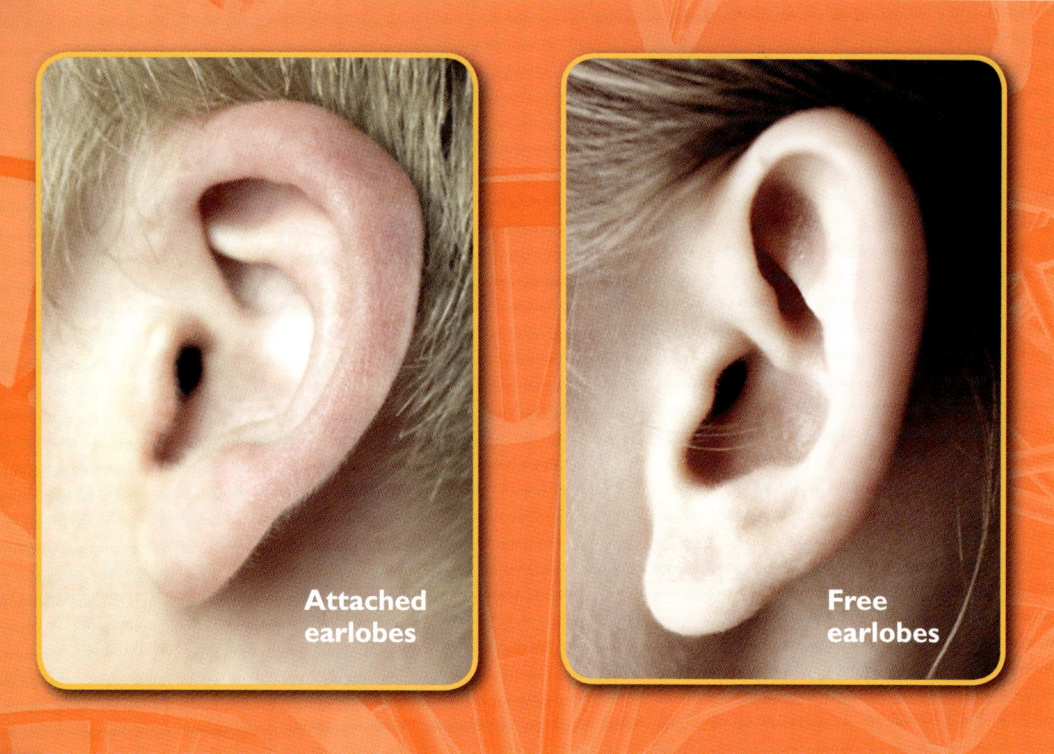

Attached earlobes

Free earlobes

Inquire and Investigate
Complete Dominance

Question: If one parent has two dominant alleles for a trait, can an offspring display the recessive trait?

Answer the question: I think that if one parent has two dominant alleles for a trait, an offspring _____.

Form a hypothesis: If one parent has two dominant alleles for a trait, an offspring (can/cannot) display the recessive trait.

Test the hypothesis:

Materials
- two small paper bags
- 15 brown M&Ms (dominant freckle alleles)
- 5 yellow M&Ms (recessive nonfreckle alleles)

Procedure
- Put 10 brown M&Ms in one bag and 5 brown and 5 yellow M&Ms in the other bag. The first bag represents a parent with two dominant freckle alleles. The second bag represents a parent with one dominant freckle allele and one recessive nonfreckle allele.

- Draw one M&M out of the first bag. Then draw one M&M out of the second bag. Set the pair aside. Continue drawing one M&M out of each bag to create allele combinations until all of the M&Ms are gone.

- Study your allele combinations. What do you notice?

Observations: Five draws will yield a brown/brown combination. The other five draws will yield a brown/yellow combination. All combinations would result in an offspring with freckles.

Conclusions: If one parent has two dominant alleles for a trait, an offspring cannot display the recessive trait. Since every possible allele combination will have at least one dominant allele, the dominant trait will always be expressed. Even if the other parent contributes a recessive allele, the first parent's dominant allele will overshadow it. This proves Mendel's theory of complete dominance.

Codominance

In some cases, the alleles of a gene for a specific trait are codominant. This means that neither allele dominates over the other. Individuals with two different codominant alleles express both forms equally and separately.

Human ABO blood-typing is an example of a trait controlled by multiple alleles, two of which are codominant when paired with each other. There are three alleles for the blood-type gene—A, B, and O. A and B are codominant. This means that when both A and B are present, neither allele dominates and the trait is determined by both (type AB blood). But when only an A or a B allele is present, that allele shows complete dominance over a recessive O allele.

All of the possible combinations of alleles result in four possible blood types: A, B, AB, and O. Do you know what type you are?

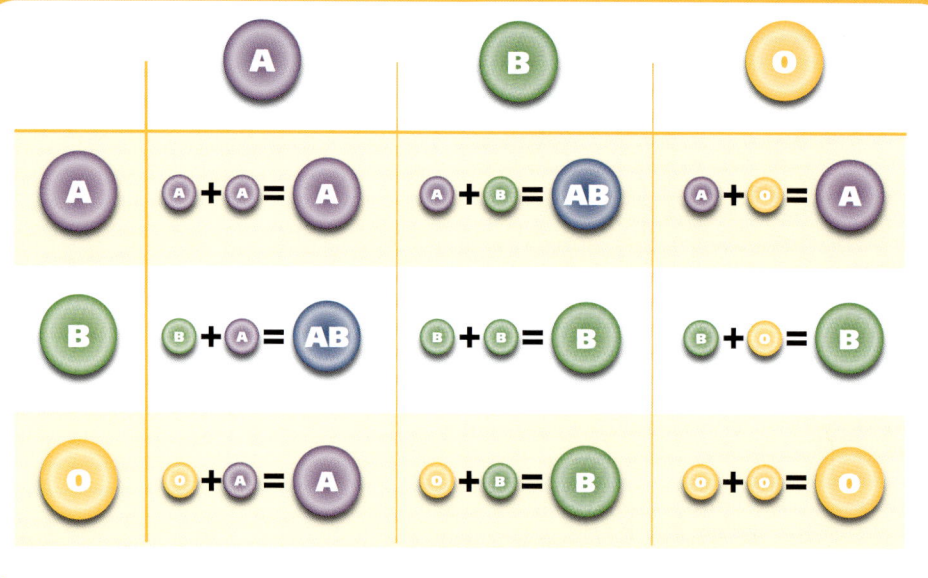

Factor In This As Well

What does it mean when someone says she has O-negative or A-positive blood? The negative or positive designation is called the *Rh factor*. Rh factor is a substance found on the red blood cells of some people. It is controlled by another gene with two alleles. The dominant form is positive (Rh factor is present), while the recessive form is negative (no Rh factor). Combining both ABO and Rh blood-typing, there are actually eight blood types: A+, A-, B+, B-, AB+, AB-, O+, and O-.

Incomplete Dominance

Incomplete dominance occurs when no allele is dominant over another. Instead, the displayed trait is a mixture of the allele traits. Hair texture in humans is due to incomplete dominance. There are two alleles for hair texture—straight and curly. Offspring who inherit two alleles for straight hair will have straight hair. Offspring with two alleles for curly hair will have curly hair. Offspring with one straight-hair allele and one curly-hair allele will have wavy hair that's neither completely straight nor really curly.

When offspring pass on their alleles, they will pass on either a straight-hair or curly-hair allele. There is no wavy-hair allele. While the trait may have taken on a blended appearance, the alleles have not blended.

X-Linked Genes

Some genes are present only on X chromosomes. These genes are called *X-linked* or *sex-linked genes*.

X-linked genes affect men more than women. This is because women have two X chromosomes, while men have only one. If a female inherits one dominant healthy allele, it will overrule a recessive "unhealthy" one. Since a male receives only one X chromosome, he doesn't have another allele to help out. He will display whatever trait is on the one allele he gets.

Color blindness is a common X-linked trait. The dominant allele carried on the X chromosome allows people to distinguish red and green. The recessive form of the allele causes red-green color blindness. Because females have two X chromosomes, they will have red-green color blindness only if they inherit two copies of the recessive allele. A male, on the other hand, will be red-green color blind if he inherits just one recessive allele from his mother.

What do you see in the circle? A person with normal vision will see the number 74. A red-green color-blind person will see the number 21. A totally color-blind person will see no number at all.

Multiple Genes

Many traits are controlled by more than one gene. That's why people aren't just tall or short. Instead, there is a wide range of heights among people. Skin and eye colors come in a variety of shades because they are determined by multiple genes.

Many Genes

The inheritance of traits from multiple genes is known as polygenic inheritance. *Polygenic* means "many genes."

Human hair color is another multiple-gene trait. Several sets of genes determine how much color is present in a person's hair. Color-producing alleles are dominant over noncolor-producing alleles. If a person has many of the color alleles in her set of hair-color genes, she will have dark hair. A person who has a majority of noncolor alleles will have fair hair. An even mix of both will produce a medium shade of brown hair.

One more gene can also appear in the mix. A person who inherits two recessive red-hair alleles will have red hair. But the shade of red depends on the color-producing genes. A person with two red alleles and a lot of color alleles will have dark auburn hair, while a person with the red alleles and very few color alleles will have light "strawberry blonde" hair.

Mutations

chapter five

The ability of DNA to duplicate itself perfectly is amazing. Once in a while, though, an error does occur. These errors are called **mutations**. Although it sounds scary, a mutation is simply a change in a gene or a chromosome.

Mutations occur for several reasons. Sometimes when genes are copying themselves, the bases match up incorrectly or in the wrong order. Other times, the chromosomes don't separate correctly during cell division and a chromosome is added or deleted. In some cases, major regions of chromosomes are rearranged.

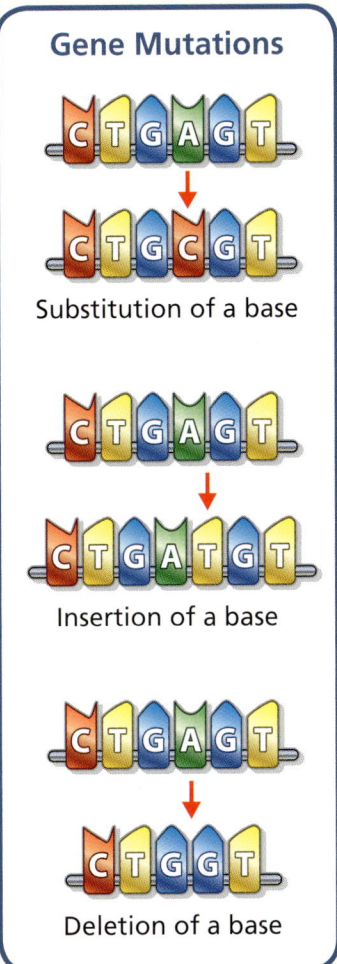

Gene Mutations

Substitution of a base

Insertion of a base

Deletion of a base

Most mutations are harmless and go unnoticed in a body. Mutations that occur in skin cells, for example, simply "go away" when the cells die and flake off the body.

Mutations are passed on only if they happen in reproductive cells (egg or sperm cells). When this occurs, every cell in the offspring's body will have the mutation. Most of these mutations are still not harmful. If a trait is the result of many genes working together, for instance, one mutated gene often has little or no effect on the overall trait.

Serious mutations result in genetic disorders. Cystic fibrosis, sickle-cell anemia, and Down syndrome are diseases caused by mutations.

Tracing the Path of Science

Hugo de Vries, one of the men who rediscovered Mendel's work, also discovered mutations. In 1886, de Vries was studying the growth of flowers called *evening primroses*. Although most of his results were similar to Mendel's, every once in a while, a new type of flower with entirely different characteristics would appear. Some of these plants would then pass on the new trait to their offspring. De Vries called these sudden changes *mutations*. He believed that mutations were responsible for the creation of new species.

In the early 1900s, Thomas Hunt Morgan experimented with fruit flies. His studies revealed that mutations occurred *within* a species. Morgan's ideas led to modern theories on mutations.

New Genetic Frontiers

chapter six

Geneticists continue to make discoveries about heredity. New areas of science have arisen from this knowledge. Genomics is the study of all of an organism's genes and how they function. Gene therapy is a new procedure used to treat genetic disorders. The genetic frontier is wide open to scientists who want to know more about heredity and how to use genetic information to make people's lives better.

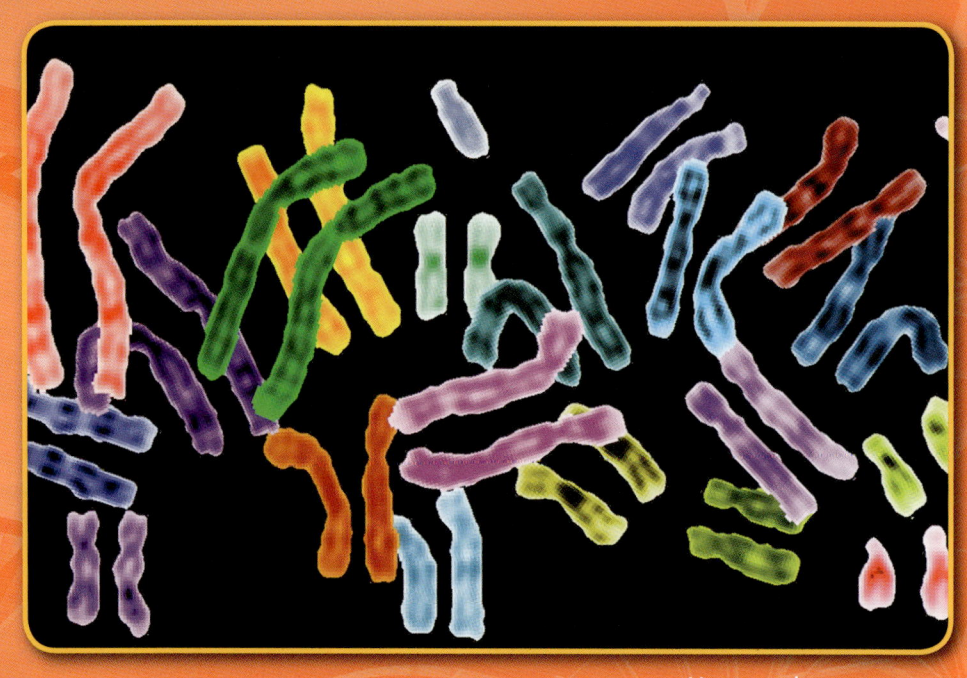

Human chromosomes

Mapping Genes

In 2003, the Human Genome Project finished mapping the location of all the genes in the human body. This complete set of genes is called a **genome**. While working on the genome map, scientists also identified many new genes. Researchers are now combing the genome to identify genes associated with different diseases and health conditions. They hope that by understanding how these disorders occur, they'll be able to find cures for them.

For example, some mutated genes increase a person's chance of developing certain cancers. Recently, the Cancer Genome Project discovered a gene linked to melanoma, the deadliest form of skin cancer. If scientists can develop a simple test for the presence of this gene, people who have it can take precautions to avoid developing the cancer. They can limit their time in the Sun, stay covered, wear sunscreen, etc. Scientists may also be able to find medicines that block the effects of the gene and prevent it from causing cancer.

Technology Link

If you've watched crime shows on television, you've seen one form of technology used to analyze genes—DNA profiling, otherwise known as DNA fingerprinting. To make DNA "fingerprints," technicians use a process called *gel electrophoresis*. The process requires a sample of a person's DNA, which can come from just about any cell in the body (skin, hair, blood, saliva, etc.). Segments of the DNA are loaded into small wells cut into a slab of gel. The gel is made from agar, which is obtained from seaweed. The gel with the DNA is placed in a box with a salt solution, and electricity is run through it. The electricity causes the DNA fragments to move down the gel. When the process is finished, the gel is stained to make the bands of DNA visible. The number and position of the bands create a genetic "fingerprint" specific to just one person.

A researcher examines a DNA sample.

Mending Genes

Gene mutations can cause inherited genetic disorders. Gene therapy is a technique for inserting working copies of a gene into a person's cells in hopes of correcting a disorder.

Scientists often use viruses to insert genes. Viruses aren't living things, but they do contain DNA or RNA. A virus causes disease by injecting its genetic material into the cells of an organism. The viral DNA or RNA forces the host cell to make more viruses. Scientists take advantage of this process by replacing viral DNA with the DNA for a specific gene. The new DNA is then placed inside cells in a body, where it can "take over" for defective genes.

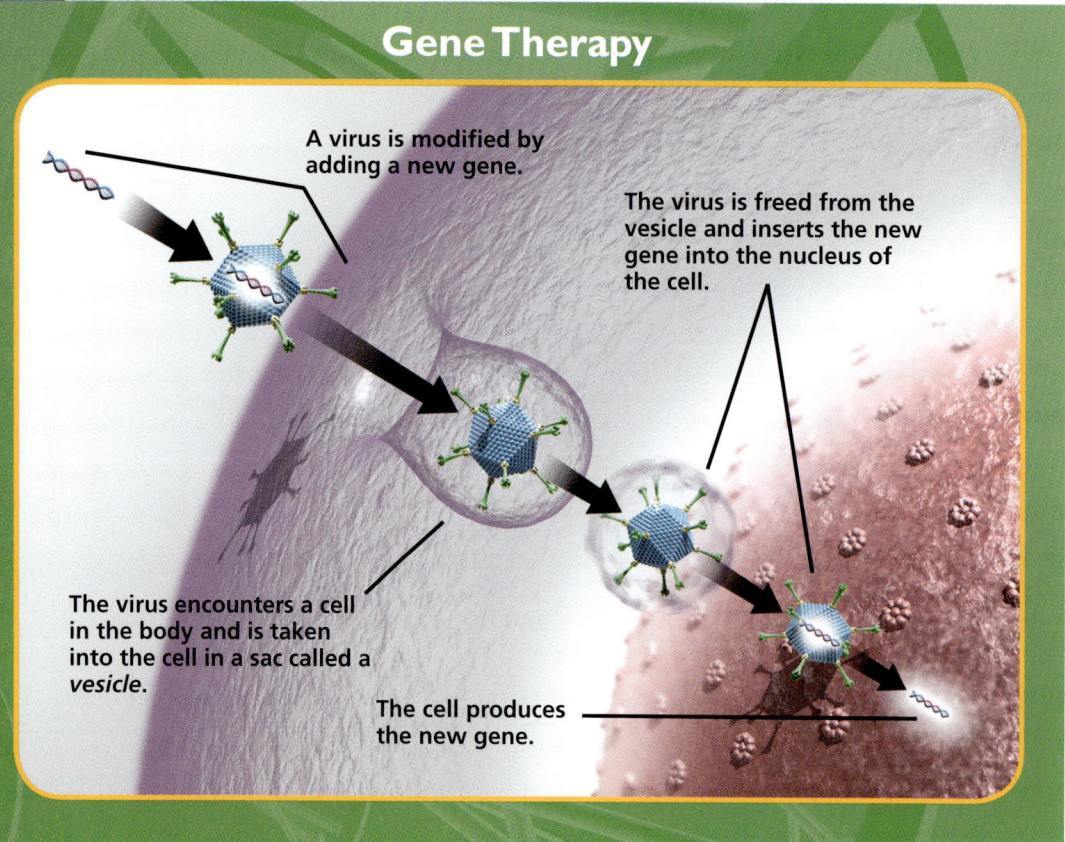

Gene Therapy

A virus is modified by adding a new gene.

The virus encounters a cell in the body and is taken into the cell in a sac called a *vesicle*.

The cell produces the new gene.

The virus is freed from the vesicle and inserts the new gene into the nucleus of the cell.

Researchers have been able to use gene therapy to treat a disease called *ADA deficiency*. People with ADA deficiency are born without working immune systems. This makes it easy for them to get very sick from everyday germs that most people can fight off. So far, doctors can treat the white blood cells that form the backbone of the immune system, but they haven't been able to treat the bone marrow cells that produce the blood cells. ADA patients require gene therapy treatments every few months.

Gene therapy has been used successfully on diseases in animals. Blindness in dogs, deafness in guinea pigs, and muscular dystrophy in mice have been cured with injections of healthy genes. These treatments may be available for humans in the future.

Gene therapy is still in its beginning stages, but it is hoped that someday it will be used to treat many human diseases.

Note: It Is Not a Permanent Fix!

Although gene therapy may cure or alleviate a genetic condition, it does not correct the original error in the person's genome. The disorder can still be passed on to future generations.

New Genetic Frontiers to Conquer

Heredity has come a long way since Mendel's pea plants. Many of the mysteries of how traits are passed on have been solved, but some are still being pursued by scientists. The mapping of the human genome has opened a whole new world for geneticists to explore. Who knows what's ahead on your genetic frontier?

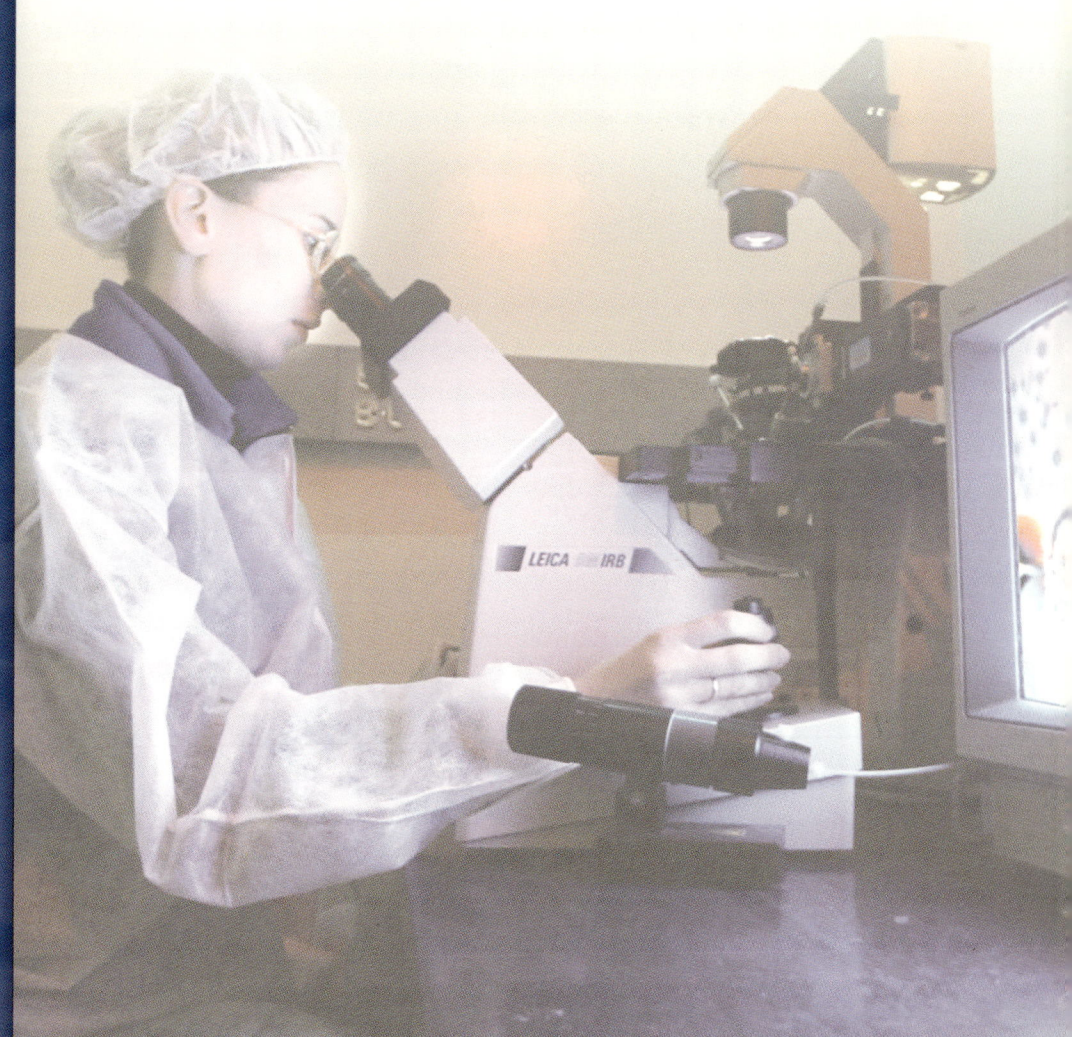

Internet Connections and Related Reading for Heredity

http://gslc.genetics.utah.edu/
Visit the Genetic Science Learning Center to review the "basics and beyond" of heredity. Then explore genetic disorders and current genetic topics.

http://www.genetics.gsk.com/kids/index_kids.htm
Fun facts, interesting information, activities, and games introduce you to DNA, genes, and heredity at this Kids Genetics site.

http://www.dnaftb.org/dnaftb/
Review and extend your knowledge of heredity with this step-by-step information provided by the Dolan DNA Learning Center.

http://library.thinkquest.org/19037/general_info.html
Attend "The Gene School" to learn more about heredity, its history, and its applications.

* * *

Coping with Hereditary Diseases by Marian Jacobs. This book examines common hereditary diseases and how to deal with them. Rosen Press, 1999. ISBN 0-8239-2823-3. [RL 8.9 IL 7–12] (3968806 HB)

Life by David Burnie. An Eyewitness Science book that explores the biology of life, including DNA, heredity, and reproduction. Dorling Kindersley, 1994. ISBN 1-5645-8477-1. [RL 8.4 IL 3–8] (5869006 HB)

- RL = Reading Level
- IL = Interest Level

Perfection Learning's catalog numbers are included for your ordering convenience. HB indicates hardback.

Glossary

allele — (uh LEEL) one form of a gene

base — (bays) one of four molecules that make up the internal structure of DNA

chromosome — (KROH muh zohm) structure inside a cell's nucleus that carries genes

crossbreed — (KRAWS breed) to produce new plants from genetically different plants

cytoplasm — (SEYE tuh plaz uhm) gel-like substance found outside a cell's nucleus

DNA — (dee en ay) deoxyribonucleic acid; molecule containing genetic information

dominant — (DAH muh nuhnt) referring to a gene or trait that is always observable if present in an organism

gene — (jeen) unit of heredity that determines traits

genetics — (juh NET iks) science of heredity

genome — (JEE nohm) complete set of genes in an organism

heredity — (huh RED uh tee) passing on of traits from one generation to the next

mutation — (myou TAY shuhn) change in a gene or chromosome

offspring (AWF spring) new organism; child

phosphate (FAHS fayt) compound formed from phosphoric acid

predisposition (pree dis puh ZISH uhn) tendency to get a disease due to heredity

protein (PROH teen) molecule in all cells that helps with growth, repair, replacement, and reproduction of cells

recessive (ree SES iv) referring to a gene or trait that is passed on but not observable when a dominant gene is present

ribosome (REYE buh sohm) part of a cell that makes proteins

RNA (ar en ay) ribonucleic acid; molecule that is a copy of genes used to make proteins

sex chromosome (seks KROH muh zohm) chromosome that determines the sex of an offspring; X and Y chromosomes in humans

trait (trayt) characteristic passed on through generations

Index

alleles, 21, 22, 24, 25, 26, 28
Aristotle, 9
Chargaff, Ernest, 17
chromosomes, 20, 29
codominance, 24
complete dominance, 22–23
Correns, Carl, 13
Crick, Francis, 15, 16, 17
de Vries, Hugo, 13, 30
DNA, 14–17, 18, 34
DNA profiling, 33
dominant genes, 12, 22
Franklin, Rosalind, 15
gene therapy, 31, 34–35
genes, 11, 14, 18–19, 20, 29, 30
genetics (definition), 7
genomics, 31
heredity
    definition, 5, 6
    history, 8–13

Human Genome Project, 32
incomplete dominance, 25
Mendel, Gregor, 10–12, 13, 21, 22
Morgan, Thomas Hunt, 30
multiple genes, 27–28
mutations, 29–30, 34
polygenic inheritance, 28
Punnett squares, 13
recessive genes, 12, 22
RNA, 18–19, 34
sex chromosomes, 20
traits (definition), 6
Tschermak, Erich, 13
Watson, James, 15, 16, 17
Wilkins, Maurice, 15
X-linked genes, 26

James Bowie Middle School
700 Plantation Drive
Richmond, TX 77406

DATE DUE		

576.5
BLE

3 3396 03422560 0
Bledsoe, Karen E.

Heredity

430149 01895   37766C   0174